LIFE ON ANCIENT EARTH

SEA MONSTERS

Julie K. Lundgren

Cherry Lake Press

Published in the United States of America by Cherry Lake Publishing Group
Ann Arbor, Michigan

www.cherrylakepublishing.com

Reading Adviser: Beth Walker Gambro, MS, Ed., Reading Consultant, Yorkville, IL

Photo Credits:
© Romolo Tavani /Shutterstock, (ocean background), cover and throughout book, © Dotted Yeti / Shutterstock, (Ichthyosaur), © Michael Rosskothen /Shutterstock, (Liopleurodon), © Warpaint /Shutterstock, (Plesiosaurus), cover; © Mj_arch/Shutterstock, colored border at bottom and top, cover and throughout book; © Art Posting/Shutterstock, background pattern art, back cover and throughout book; © mentalmind/ Shutterstock, (rock sidebar art throughout book); © Maquiladora/Shutterstock, (small illustration, top left on all MEET A MONSTER pages); © We Little Birds/Shutterstock, page 4; © Liliya Butenko/Shutterstock, (top), © Aunt Spray/Shutterstock, (bottom), page 5; © Mihai_Andritoiu/Shutterstock, (top), © BlueRingMedia/ Shutterstock, (bottom), page 6; © Marycaroline91/Shutterstock, (hand), © Jonathon Kosec/Shutterstock, (shark teeth on beach), page 7; © DiBgd.Creative Commons Attribution-Share Alike 4.0 International, (drawing), © Igor Kovalchuk/Shutterstock, (jaws), page 8; © Warpaint/Shutterstock, page 9; © Michael Rosskothen/Shutterstock, page 10; © Chonmapoom Phaisri | Dreamstime, (bottom), © William Roberts | Dreamstime.com, (top), © Chonmapoom Phaisri | Dreamstime.com, (bottom), page 11; © Steve Allen/ Shutterstock, pages 12-13; © Hada Arkanda | Dreamstime.com, page 14; © Daniel Eskridge/Shutterstock, page 15; © Norbert Dr. Lange | Dreamstime.com, (top), © Dotted Yeti/Shutterstock, (bottom), page 16; © Catmando/Shutterstock, page 17; © Somchet Nukeaw | Dreamstime.com, (top), © Reimar/Shutterstock, editorial use only, (bottom), page 18; © Dotted Yeti/Shutterstock, page 19; © Faviel_Raven/Shutterstock, editorial use only, (top), © Branislav Kapetanovic | Dreamstime.com, (bottom), page 20; © racksuz/ Shutterstock, page 21; © Artem Avetisyan/Shutterstock, (Megalodon), © W. Scott McGill/Shutterstock, (Megalodon tooth), © Marko Aliaksandr/Shutterstock, (asteroid), page 22; © CLOUD-WALKER/Shutterstock, page 23.

Produced for Cherry Lake Publishing by bluedooreducation.com

Cherry Lake Press is an imprint of Cherry Lake Publishing Group.

Library of Congress Cataloging-in-Publication Data has been filed and is available at catalog.loc.gov.

Printed in the United States of America

ABOUT THE AUTHOR

Julie K. Lundgren once went fossil hunting with her family. They found many fossil corals and shells in an old quarry! *Adventures await* is her motto. Julie's interest in nature and science led her to a degree in biology. She lives in Minnesota with her family and sweet, green-eyed cat.

CONTENTS

TURN BACK NOW!

Swoosh back in time to long ago. Before people. Before the rise of mammals.

Warm, salty seas covered much of Earth back then. The air was warm everywhere. Earth's poles had no ice or snow.

At the time of big land dinosaurs, giant life forms also ruled the seas.

THE SOUP OF LIFE

Animals and plants thrived in **ancient** seas. Rich in all they needed to live, the seas fed them. Over the ages, more life forms grew. They got bigger, too.

How do we know this? From **fossils**! Animal and plant fossils found in rock layers help tell Earth's story.

Fossil layers are like a book of time. Older fossils lie in deeper layers than younger fossils. Scientists name each major layer or era as if they are chapters.

DIG THIS!

In Venice, Florida, ancient shark teeth wash up on the beach. Fossil hunters sift sand through a fine net to find them.

The fossil record tells us that giant creatures once filled the seas. Let's dive into Earth's prehistoric seas and look for these prehistoric monsters!

PALEOZOIC PREDATORS

The Paleozoic Era had sharks and other toothy swimmers. These hunters turned good days into nightmares for their prey.

Stethacanthus lived about 350 million years ago. The top of its head and its strange fin felt like toothbrush bristles.

Predators' teeth cut like knives, scissors, and blenders. Those chompers made it impossible for prey to wiggle free.

MEET A MONSTER: ORTHACANTHUS

What do you get when you cross a giant eel with a swamp shark? A bad dream? Yes, and it's a sea monster named *Orthacanthus*! This slithery swimmer had a long fin along its spine. It lurked among weedy plants to sneak up on prey. It used its sharp teeth to grip slippery fish and other animals.

Name: *Orthacanthus*
Pronunciation: or-thuh-KAN-thus
Lived: About 280 million years ago
Length: Almost 10 feet (3 meters)

MEET A MONSTER: EDESTUS

Meet *Edestus*! This ancient shark had a line of teeth on the roof and bottom of its mouth like scissors. When its jaws clamped prey, its teeth sank deep. *Edestus* then whipped its head up and down to rip the meat. What a messy eater!

Name: *Edestus*
Pronunciation: ee-DESS-tuhs
Lived: 300 million years ago
Length: Almost 20 feet (6 m)

These predators didn't last. Earth changed over time. A **mass extinction** ended the Paleozoic Era. Big and small, most sea life died. So long, sea scorpions! Goodbye, *Edestus*!

sea scorpion

These mini monsters were never found again in the fossil record.

What happened on Earth? Gases changed the oceans. Sea animals could not get enough oxygen or find food. That's why nearly all sea life died.

DEEP TIME: MASS EXTINCTION

During this mass extinction, huge volcanoes spewed ash and killer gases into the air. Ash and gases acted like a blanket over Earth. Trapped heat changed the **climate**. This mass extinction was like 4 million volcanoes erupting!

MEGA MONSTERS

After the mass extinction, some animals still lived. The Mesozoic Era began. New animals developed.

DEEP TIME: 252 MILLION TO 66 MILLION YEARS AGO

On land, dinosaurs ruled the Mesozoic Era. At the same time, the oceans had the biggest sea monsters. It was a scary time to be alive!

MEET A MONSTER: SHASTASAURUS

About 210 million years ago lived one of the biggest sea reptiles of all time. Shaped like a huge dolphin, *Shastasaurus* swam well. It had no teeth. Instead, it sucked prey into its mouth.

Name: *Shastasaurus*
Pronunciation: shas-tuh-SOR-uss
Lived: About 210 million years ago
Length: Almost 70 feet (21 m)

Over time, many sea monsters developed. One group of monsters was called **plesiosaurs**. They had long necks and large flippers.

Elasmosaurus, a type of plesiosaurus, poked its head above the water to breathe.

Name: *Elasmosaurus*
Pronunciation: ee-lazz-mo-SORE-uss
Lived: About 90 million years ago
Length: About 46 feet (14 m)

MEET A MONSTER: LIOPLEURODON

Time travel back 160 million years ago to meet *Liopleurodon*. It looked a bit like a crocodile with flippers. This **apex predator** could smell prey. It hunted giant fish and sea reptiles.

Name: *Liopleurodon*
Pronunciation: LEE-oh-PLOOR-ch-don
Lived: About 160 million years ago
Length: Almost 26 feet (8 m)

Turn back time 100 million to 66 million years ago to find the mosasaurs.

Mosasaurs lived at the same time as plesiosaurs. Some ate big sea reptiles and fish. Others crunched on animals with shells.

MEET A MONSTER: MOSASAURUS

This apex predator gave its prey a five-alarm fright. Its huge jaws crushed. Its many teeth sliced. It **ambushed** prey. Sleek and large, it ruled Earth's seas.

Name: *Mosasaurus*
Pronunciation: moh-zuh-SOR-uss
Lived: About 80 million years ago
Length: 56 feet (17 m)

This is a fossil skeleton of an ichthyosaur. Ichthyosaurs lived alongside plesiosaurs. But they went extinct about 90 million years ago.

How do we know what these sea monsters ate? Fossils of their prey are sometimes found inside them! Fossils found nearby also give us clues.

DEEP TIME: MASS EXTINCTION

Underwater volcanoes and **asteroids** killed off plesiosaurs 66 million years ago.

MEET A MONSTER: PREDATOR X

A fossil of Predator X was found above the Arctic Circle. This place was not cold and icy in the time of Predator X. Everything about Predator X made it a nightmare:

- Teeth like needles
- Crushing jaws
- Strong fins and tail
- Massive size: 12 tons (11 metric tons)

Name: Predator X
Pronunciation: PREH-dah-tor EKS
Lived: About 150 million years ago
Length: Up to 42 feet (12 m)

Megalodon lived after the age of dinosaurs. At almost 79 feet (24 m), it topped all sharks in size. It became extinct 3.6 million years ago.

DEEP TIME: 66 MILLION YEARS AGO

A huge asteroid hit Earth causing a worldwide climate shift. Many dinosaurs and other animals on land and sea died out.

GEOLOGIC TIMELINE

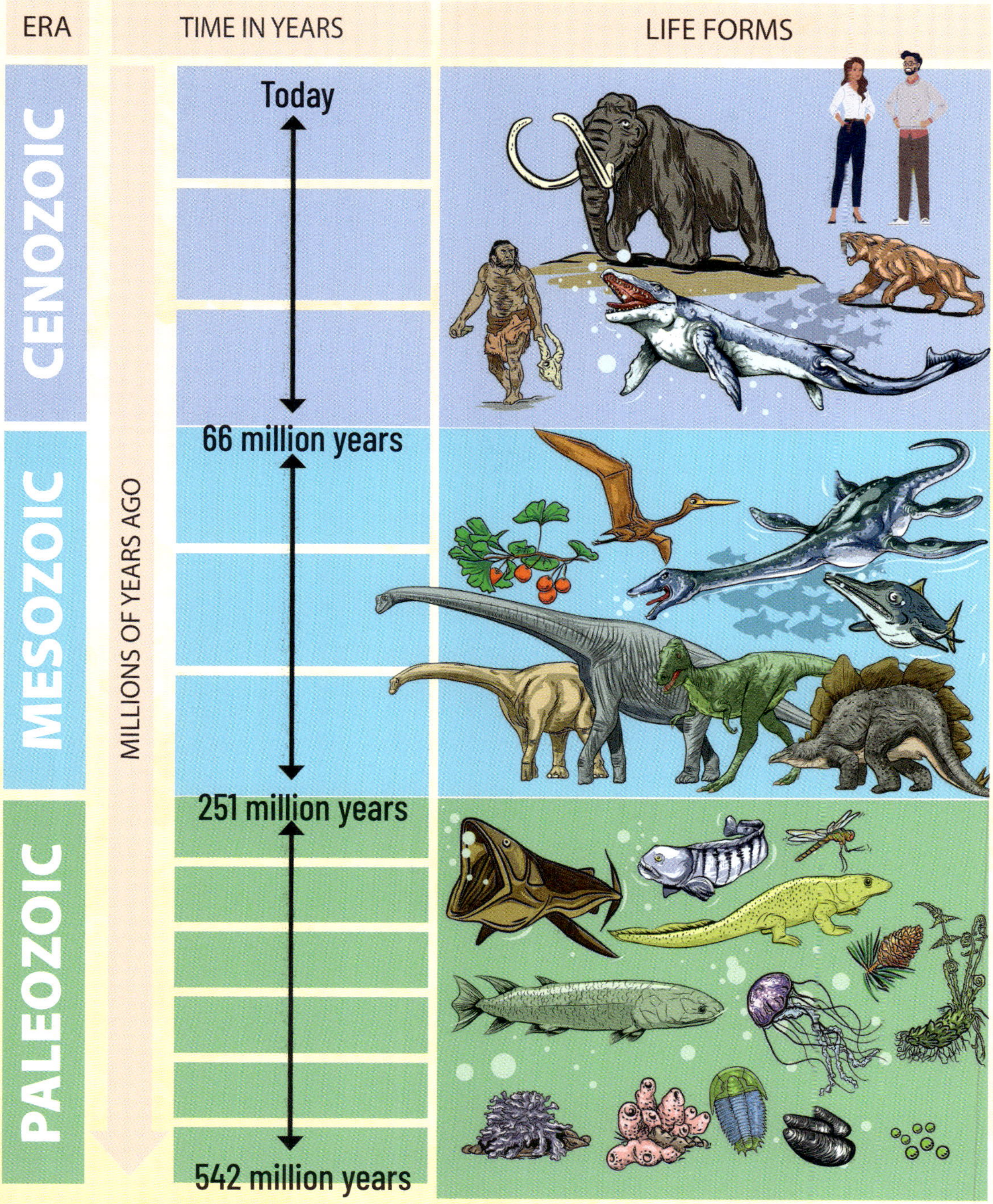

Scientists divide Earth's history into eras to help them organize Earth's past and study how life has changed. Each section marks important events, like when new life appeared or when many plants and animals went extinct.

FIND OUT MORE

BOOKS

Naish, Darren. *Ancient Sea Reptiles: Plesiosaurs, Ichthyosaurs, Mosasaurs, and More.* Washington, DC: Smithsonian Books, 2023.

Warren Drimmer, Stephanie. *Prehistoric Sea Monsters.* London, UK: National Geographic Kids, Harper Collins, 2024.

WEBSITES

Search these online sources with an adult:

National Geographic Kids | Megalodon

Natural History Museum, UK | The Rise of The Dinosaurs

GLOSSARY

ambushed (AM-bushed) attacked by surprise

ancient (AYN-schent) belonging to a time long ago

apex predator (AY-peks PREH-dah-ter) a hunter animal with no predators that hunt it

asteroid (AS-tuh-royd) a chunk of rock or metal from space that hits Earth

climate (KLAHY-meht) the overall weather of an area over long periods of time

fossils (FAH-sulz) the hard remains or shapes of plants or animals from long ago

mass extinction (MASS eks-TINK-shun) a violent event that kills most of life on Earth

plesiosaurs (PLEE-zee-uh-sorz) a group of prehistoric sea reptiles in the Mesozoic Era

INDEX